W9-AQB-680

THE UNTAMED WORLD

Grizzly Bears

Janice Parker

RSVP

RAINTREE
STECK-VAUGHN
PUBLISHERS
The Steck-Vaughn Company

Austin, Texas

1539 7944

Published by Raintree Steck-Vaughn Publishers, an imprint of Steck-Vaughn Company.

Library of Congress Cataloging-in-Publication Data
Parker, Janice.
    Grizzly bears / Janice Parker.
        p.   cm. -- (The Untamed world)
    Includes bibliographical references (p. 63) and index.
    Summary: Examines the habitat, food, social activities,
and folklore of the grizzly bear.
    ISBN 0-8172-4563-4
    1. Grizzly bear--Juvenile literature.   [1. Grizzly bear.
2. Bears.] I. Title. II. Series.
II. Series.
QL737.C27P355   1997
599.74'446--dc20
                      96-2834
                      CIP
                      AC

Printed and bound in Canada
1234567890 01 00 99 98 97

Project Editor
Lauri Seidlitz

Design and Illustration
Warren Clark

Project Coordinator
Amanda Woodrow

Raintree Steck-Vaughn Publishers Editor
Kathy DeVico

Copyeditor
Janice Parker

Layout
Chris Bowerman

Consultant
Peter Clarkson, Wolf and Brown Bear Biologist, and Executive Director of the Gwich'in Renewable Resource Board, N.W.T., Canada

Acknowledgments
The publisher wishes to thank Warren Rylands for inspiring this series.

Photograph Credits

Calgary Zoological Society: pages 5 (Patrick McCloskey), 15 (Brian Keating), 25 (Rosemary Dunne); **Corel Corporation**: cover, pages 4, 7, 8, 14, 16, 18, 28, 29, 42, 59, 60, 61; **John Downey**: page 33; **Eastern Slopes Grizzly Bear Project**: pages 41 (Paczowski), 54 (Gibeau); **Ivy Images**: pages 10 (J.D. Taylor), 17, 34, 37, 40 (Gary Crandall), 24 (Robert McCaw), 44; **National Park Service**: pages 27 bottom, 35, 43, 57; **Parks Canada**: pages 6, 22 (W. Lynch); **Tom Stack and Associates**: pages 20 (Barbara von Hoffmann), 21 (John Shaw), 9, 23 (Thomas Kitchin), 32 (John Shaw); **Valhalla Society**: page 56 (W. McCrory); **Visuals Unlimited**: pages 26 (Beth Davidow), 27 top, 36 (Joe McDonald); **John C. Whyte**: page 30.

Contents

Introduction

Folklore commonly describes the grizzly as a powerful animal that people both fear and admire.

Opposite: The fur of some grizzlies can look white or silver in the sunshine, giving these bears their nickname, "silvertips."

Many people are surprised to find out that grizzlies can be playful and relaxed.

Some people believe that grizzlies are vicious animals that attack humans for no reason. Even the name "grizzly bear" suggests a ferocious, fearsome beast. In reality, while grizzly bears are able to use their strength, teeth, and claws to defend themselves and to get food, they prefer to stay as far away from humans as possible.

This book will show you where the grizzly bear lives, what it eats, and how it spends its winters. You will also read about grizzly cubs, and how they survive their first years of life. Find out why the grizzly is in danger of disappearing from parts of the United States and Canada, and what you can do to help.

Many legends and stories have been written about the grizzly bear. Folklore commonly describes the grizzly as a powerful animal that people both fear and admire. Some cultures call this animal "grandfather," while one culture will not even say the name of the grizzly out loud.

This book takes a close look at the grizzly bear in its natural habitat, and helps you decide how you feel about the grizzly.

Features

Grizzly bears are very well adapted for their sometimes harsh environment.

Opposite: The grizzly bear's long claws are used mostly for digging in the soil for food, and for digging dens.

Grizzly bears are larger than most of the other animals in their habitat. They can weigh more than six adult humans, and they have long claws at the ends of large, strong paws. If you have ever been lucky enough to see a grizzly bear in the wild, you may have noticed its large size, but you probably did not see it closely enough to notice any other details. At a quick glance, a grizzly may easily be mistaken for another type of bear, such as the black bear. As you learn more about the grizzly, however, you will discover many ways to distinguish it from other bears.

Grizzly bears are very well adapted for their sometimes harsh environment. They are able to survive cold winters, eat whatever food is available, and defend themselves against the other animals that share their territory. These special features give grizzlies their nickname, "King of the Wilderness."

The grizzly's large shoulder hump of fat and muscle is one of the best ways to tell a grizzly bear apart from a black bear.

Size

Grizzly bears vary greatly in size, depending on whether the bear is male or female, its age, and where it lives. Adult male grizzly bears can weigh anywhere from 300 to more than 800 pounds (136 to 363 kg), and can be 6 to 7 feet (1.8 to 2.1 m) long from head to tail. Female grizzlies are 40 percent smaller than male grizzlies. They weigh about 200 to 500 pounds (91 to 227 kg) when full-grown.

Grizzlies that live in areas where there is plenty of high-protein food, such as salmon, are often much larger than bears that eat mainly leaves, grasses, roots, and berries.

All grizzly bears are at their largest and fattest in late summer and early fall. At this time, the bears eat enormous amounts of food in preparation for entering their winter den. Once inside their dens, grizzlies do not normally eat until spring. Over the winter, female grizzlies with cubs may lose 30 percent or more of their body weight.

LIFE SPAN

The average life span of a grizzly bear is 25 years, but some wild grizzlies have lived for as long as 30 years. Grizzlies in captivity do not have to face the dangers and difficulties of the wild. Some captive grizzlies have lived for more than 44 years.

It is not always possible to tell a male grizzly bear from a female grizzly bear by comparing their size. The picture above shows a similar-sized male and female during mating season. The male is probably a younger bear.

Fur

Although grizzly bears are a type of brown bear, their fur can be several different colors, including off-white or almost black. The fur of a brown-colored grizzly is often different shades of brown on different parts of its body. Some grizzly bears have fur with white or silver tips on the ends, which gives them a **grizzled** appearance. This is how the grizzly bear gets its name.

The grizzly bear has two types of fur. The **underfur** is a short, soft, fine hair that is close to the bear's skin. The **guard hairs** are what we see when we look at a bear. They are longer and coarser than the underfur.

These two layers of fur work very well together. They insulate the grizzly from the heat and the cold, and they protect the bear's skin from insects, dirt, and the sun. Fur helps to **camouflage** the bear in its natural habitat, and is sometimes used as a form of communication. For example, an angry bear may raise the fur on its shoulders to appear more threatening.

Grizzlies **molt** once a year during late spring and early summer. This means that they shed their thick outer fur to reveal their shorter, cooler underfur. During this time, grizzlies rub against trees and rocks to help remove the old hair. When the bears are molting, they look very ragged and messy. Molting takes only a few weeks, and after molting, the grizzly bear has a shiny, sleek coat of fur. When colder weather approaches, grizzlies grow a thick new coat of longer fur to prepare them for winter.

Although the fur of some grizzlies can look silvery in bright sunlight, most bears are well camouflaged. The brownish-colored fur of the grizzly bear can make it very difficult to see from a distance.

Special Adaptations

Grizzly bears have many features that help them survive the challenges of their environment.

A grizzly bear may show its teeth and jaws to frighten off intruders. Although the teeth of a grizzly can look very threatening, they are most often used for chewing up the plants that they eat.

Canine teeth for eating meat

Molars for chewing plants

Hearing and Vision

For many years, people believed that grizzly bears had poor eyesight. Recent evidence now shows that their vision is as good as human eyesight. Grizzlies also have excellent hearing. Scientists believe that grizzly bears can hear the movements of ground squirrels underneath several inches of soil.

Smell

Many wildlife biologists believe that grizzlies have a better sense of smell than any other North American animal. It is their most important sense. Grizzlies can smell food sources that are several miles away! They also use their sense of smell to locate mates during mating season, to identify cubs, and to avoid humans.

Teeth

Grizzly bears have 42 teeth and very powerful jaws. Along with its paws and claws, a grizzly's teeth are its main tools for defense and for obtaining food. Grizzly bears have long, sharp canine teeth in the fronts of their mouths for eating meat. They also have flat molars that are used for chewing plant food.

Paws

A grizzly bear uses its paws for walking, swimming, killing prey, feeding, digging, lifting, pulling, turning, and self-defense. A grizzly's paws look very big and awkward, but they are actually able to gently hold and move small objects, such as stones and berry branches.

Shoulders

The shoulder, or "hump," on the back of the grizzly bear helps people to distinguish grizzlies from black bears. The hump is made of fat and very strong muscles. With these strong shoulder muscles, a grizzly can knock down a moose or an elk with just one swipe of a paw.

Claws

At the end of each paw are five toes with **nonretractable** claws. This means the claws are fixed in an outstretched position and cannot be pulled in like the claws of a cat. A grizzly's claws grow up to 6 inches (15 cm) in length, and can be dark or light in color. Sometimes people are not sure whether they have seen grizzly bear tracks or black bear tracks. Here are some ways that you can tell the difference between the two:

Grizzly bear

- Tracks can be very large.
- Claw marks are visible.
- Claws are 2–3 inches (5–7.6 cm) ahead of the toe marks.

Black bear

- Tracks are smaller.
- Claw marks are not always visible.
- If present, claw marks are closer to the footprint.

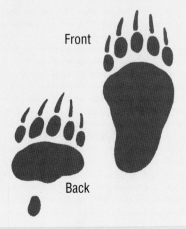

Front

Back

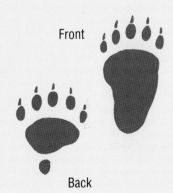

Front

Back

Classification

Most wildlife biologists agree that there are eight different species of bears in the world. Despite their differences, all bears share many similarities. They all have large, heavy bodies, short tails, thick fur, large heads, and rounded ears. All bears walk on flat feet, and have a good sense of smell. They are all strong, intelligent, independent, and they spend a lot of time alone.

Brown bears
Eastern and Western Europe, Northern Asia, Japan, Western Canada, Alaska, and some western states

Polar bears
Arctic

Giant Pandas
Southwestern China

American black bears
Forested areas of North America

Sun bears
Southeast Asia

BEARS OF THE WORLD

Asiatic black bears
Southern Asia

Spectacled bears
Mountains in South America

Sloth bears
India and Sri Lanka

Brown Bears

The grizzly bear is just one of the many types of brown bears found in North America, Europe, and Asia. At one time, scientists thought there were many different species of brown bears. They now believe that all brown bears are part of the same species: *Ursus arctos*. *Ursus* means "bear" in Latin, and *arctos* means "bear" in Greek, so the scientific name for the brown bear is "bear bear."

SUBSPECIES

In order to describe the differences among various brown bears, scientists divided them into groups called subspecies. The grizzly bear (*Ursus arctos horribilus*) is one subspecies. There is another brown bear subspecies that also lives in North America. It is called the Kodiak brown bear (*Ursus arctos middendorffi*). It lives only on Kodiak Island, Alaska, and some of the surrounding islands. Here is a list of some well-known subspecies of the brown bear, and where they live:

Subspecies	Latin Name	Where They Live
Brown bear	*Ursus arctos arctos*	North America, Europe, Asia
Grizzly bear	*Ursus arctos horribilus*	United States, Canada
Red bear	*Ursus arctos isabellinus*	India, Himalayas
Black grizzly	*Ursus arctos lasiotus*	China, Mongolia
Kodiak brown bear	*Ursus arctos middendorffi*	Alaska (Kodiak, and surrounding islands)
Mexican grizzly bear	*Ursus arctos nelsoni*	Mexico
Yezo brown bear	*Ursus arctos yesoensis*	Hokkaido, Japan

Social Activities

Grizzlies do not usually waste time fighting when they could be eating instead.

Grizzly bears like to live alone. They avoid other bears, and consider other animals only as a source of food. Grizzlies need to spend so much of their time eating that they will avoid almost any situation that does not lead to a meal. Generally peaceful animals, bears usually choose easy meals over food that involves a lot of work and conflict. Grizzlies do not usually waste time fighting when they could be eating instead.

Opposite: It is very unusual to see more than one grizzly bear at the same time, unless you see a mother and her cubs.

Younger bears spend much of their time playing and learning with other cubs or their mother.

Home Ranges

Grizzly bears spend most of their active period, during spring, summer, and fall, in search of food. Within a grizzly habitat, each bear has its own neighborhood, or **home range**. An ideal home range is an area with lots of food and good locations for dens. Male grizzly bears have larger home ranges than females. The home range of a female grizzly may be 100 square miles (260 sq km) or less, while the home range of a male grizzly may be as large as 1,500 square miles (3,900 sq km). Grizzlies spend the entire winter in their dens. During the rest of the year, they spend most of their time traveling throughout their home ranges in search of food sources.

The home range of one grizzly often overlaps with the ranges of other grizzlies. Grizzlies usually try to avoid one another, however, and leave markings so that others know they are in the area. Adult male grizzlies will chase away any other male grizzlies who enter their home range.

Grizzlies have a strong homing instinct. If they are captured by scientists and released outside their range, they will usually find their way back to their range in a very short time period.

A Sloth of Bears

A group of bears in one place almost always means that there is a lot of food around. The most common place to see a sloth of bears is at a good fishing area.

A group of bears is called a sloth. It is uncommon to see grizzly bears in groups. There are only a few times when a grizzly bear will accept the presence of another bear. During mating season in the spring, male and female grizzly bears will spend 1 or 2 weeks together. Grizzly cubs will spend their first few years with their mother. After leaving their mother, older cubs often spend their first season together before they each find new homes. Grizzlies will also gather to feast at particularly good food sources.

Bears that live near the coast will eat large amounts of salmon during the summer. From June to October, salmon swim upstream from the ocean to rivers and streams to lay their eggs. There are so many salmon at this time that grizzly bears will stay near the streams and eat as much as possible. During the salmon season, as many as 15 grizzly bears have been seen fishing in one area of a river. There is so much salmon that grizzlies do not have to compete for food, so they put up with the presence of other grizzlies.

Seasonal Activities

In late spring, summer, and fall, grizzly bears spend most of their time trying to fatten up for winter. They often travel long distances in search of food.

Throughout the day, grizzlies may stop to sleep on the ground, or in a daybed. Daybeds can be grassy areas, or shallow holes in the ground that are lined with leaves and pine needles. Grizzlies have several daybeds in their home range. The daybeds are usually located near food sources, and usually have a good view of the surrounding area.

During this period, there is very little food available. In order to survive, grizzly bears make or find a safe place to sleep during the coldest months. Some people call this winter sleep **hibernation**. Many biologists, however, do not think that grizzlies truly hibernate. They call the grizzly bear's time in a den a winter dormant period.

During this period, the bear's whole body works more slowly to conserve energy. A grizzly bear breathes only 3 to 4 times per minute. In addition, its heart slows from 98 beats per minute to only 8 to 10 beats per minute. While in their den, grizzly bears do not eat, drink, or eliminate any waste. Instead, they survive by using the nutrients from their layers of fat. It is common for the bears to wake up and move around in their dens. Grizzly bears may even leave their dens if the weather is very warm, or if they are disturbed.

Grizzly bears spend their winter in a den because their food sources disappear, not because of the cold. The grizzly's thick fur and layer of fat keep it warm all winter.

The Den

A den is where a grizzly spends the winter. Most grizzlies dig their dens, often on a hillside, or on the bank of a lake or river. Adult grizzlies always go into a den alone, although mothers will share a den with their cubs. Young grizzlies that have recently left their mothers will sometimes share a den with their siblings.

A grizzly's den is not much bigger than the bear itself. Once inside the den, the grizzly bear has only enough room to stretch and turn around. This helps the bear stay warm. The grizzly bear's body heat keeps the den warm all winter.

Grizzly dens are often covered by thick layers of snow during the winter. This helps to insulate the den and keep the bear warm. There is always an air passage to the outside of the den. This means that the bear can have fresh air all winter. The entrance to the den is usually sheltered from strong winds.

It takes a grizzly bear a few weeks to fully recover from its winter sleep. Their first task is to find some food to eat. They move slowly, and often must travel long distances to find green grass to eat.

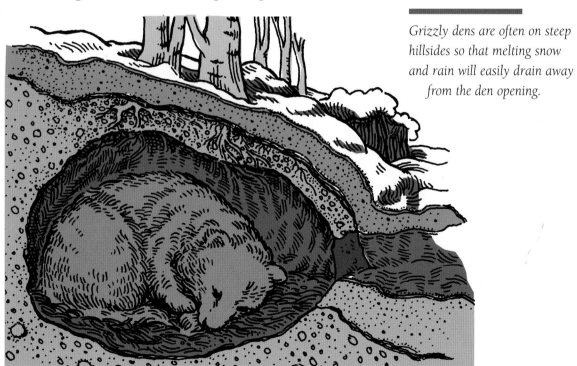

Grizzly dens are often on steep hillsides so that melting snow and rain will easily drain away from the den opening.

Communication

Some animals must communicate constantly with one another, like wolves living in packs. Animals that live in groups use sounds to warn other group members of danger, and to help keep order within their group. In contrast, grizzly bears usually live by themselves, so they do not have as much need to communicate through sounds. They have different methods for sending messages to other bears, other animals, and even humans.

Sounds

Grizzlies are generally very quiet animals, although they will grunt, snort, growl, and even roar to make their presence known. Young bear cubs will whine and squeal to communicate with their mother.

Markings

Grizzlies may also communicate through markings. Markings are signs of a bear's presence in the area. A grizzly scents an area by rubbing its body against the ground, a tree, or a rock. Grizzlies also mark an area when they urinate, leave behind droppings, or scratch the bark off tall trees. These kinds of markings let others know a grizzly is in the area.

A grizzly will rub its back on a tree to let other animals know it is in the area, or to rub off some of its winter coat of fur.

Body Language

Bears often communicate through body language. If they are angry or uncomfortable, they may open their mouths, lower their heads, raise their noses, or flatten their ears. An aggressive grizzly will stare at an intruder, or will "bluff." This means it will charge as if it is going to attack, only to stop and turn away before reaching the intruder. A grizzly mother with her cubs may warn an intruder to stay away by simply turning her body sideways.

If two bears see one another in the distance, they communicate through their actions. The smaller of the two bears usually runs away from the larger. If the bears are almost the same size, they will slowly approach each other and circle around until they decide who is bigger. Usually one bear will give up and run away.

A bear standing on its hind legs does not necessarily mean it is going to attack, or that it is aggressive. Grizzlies, especially younger bears, will often stand on their hind legs to get a better view and smell something in the area.

Grizzly Cubs

Grizzly cubs are completely helpless at birth.

Opposite: Grizzly cubs learn everything they need to know about survival by imitating their mother. This cub may be standing against its mother to get a better look at something that has caught her attention.

It can be hard to remember that grizzly cubs are wild animals with a very protective, dangerous mother.

Young bear cubs are very small, playful, and full of curiosity. It is hard to imagine that these fuzzy little cubs grow so quickly into powerful adult grizzlies. A grizzly cub can gain up to 200 pounds (91 kg) in its first year!

Grizzly cubs are completely helpless at birth. They must depend on their mothers for food, warmth, education, and protection.

Birth

Mating occurs in late spring or early summer, but grizzly cubs are not born until the following January. Although there are many months between mating and the birth of the cubs, the **gestation period** of a female grizzly is only about 3 months. The reason for the difference in time is a process called **delayed implantation**. This means that cubs will only be born if the mother has eaten enough food in late summer and early autumn. Only a well-fed grizzly bear has enough fat to provide the warmth and nourishment that she and her cubs will need in the winter months. Delayed implantation is an important survival mechanism for bears. It allows only the healthiest females to give birth to healthy cubs. It also means that in the fall when there is more food available, the bears can focus on eating rather than mating.

A female grizzly bear usually gives birth to two cubs, but she may have only one cub, or more rarely, up to four cubs. At birth, grizzly bear cubs are tiny, blind, and completely helpless. They are less than 1 foot (.3 m) long from the tips of their noses to the ends of their tails, and weigh less than 1 pound (.4 kg). Their eyes are closed shut, and they do not have any teeth. They are covered with very fine, pale hair, but they look as if they are completely bald!

Cubs born to this fattened female grizzly will have a good chance of survival.

Care

Grizzly cubs are raised entirely by their mother. In their first months in the den, the cubs rely on their mother for warmth and food. The mother's milk is very high in fat and protein. It provides the cubs with all the nutrients they need to survive. By late April to late May, if the weather has warmed up enough, the grizzly mother and her cubs leave the den to search for fresh food.

The family remains near the den until the cubs are older and stronger. The cubs gain strength by playing and exploring near their den. This prepares them for the long journeys they will make with their mother while she looks for food.

Cubs stay very close to their mother. By watching and imitating her, they learn how to find food, how to hunt, and how to build a den. They also learn how to avoid danger. The cubs' survival depends on learning these important lessons from their mother.

Grizzly cubs are very curious and playful. They spend much of their time exploring, tumbling in the grass, and playing with their cub mates. When their mother goes to sleep, the cubs often sleep right on top of her. Grizzly mothers are very gentle and patient with their lively cubs, and they are fiercely protective.

Young grizzly cubs stay very close to their mother. They rely on her for warmth and protection.

Development

For the first few months outside of the den, young grizzly cubs continue to drink their mother's milk. The position of this female grizzly allows her to watch for danger while her cubs are feeding.

Birth – 4 Months

The cubs spend their first months with their mother in the den. Within a couple of weeks, their eyes open, they get their first teeth, and they grow a coat of soft fur. The cubs grow quickly, gaining up to 8 pounds (3.6 kg) in these first months.

5 – 6 Months

The cubs become more active and curious. As the weather gets warmer, they start to wander outside the den with their mother. Cubs continue to drink their mother's milk throughout this time. By six months, when they leave the den for good, they weigh as much as 8 to 30 pounds (4 to 14 kg).

7 – 9 Months

The cubs continue to grow very quickly. By the fall, they weigh anywhere from 50 to more than 100 pounds (23 to 45 kg). During this period, they are **weaned** off their mother's milk, although some bears will continue to nurse for several more months. Grizzly cubs remain with their mothers for at least 2 years. Sometimes, however, they will stay with her for up to 4 years before going off on their own. A grizzly will not be ready to mate until it is about five years old.

One of the most important lessons that grizzly cubs learn is what to eat. This cub would have learned how to catch fish from its mother.

Habitat

Grizzlies eat just about anything, which means they can live anyplace where there is enough space and enough food.

Opposite: Many grizzlies live in remote mountain areas that will allow them enough space to avoid humans.

Grizzly bears like to live in large areas. They can live in a variety of different habitats, including coastal areas, river valleys, grasslands, wilderness forests, and mountain meadows. Grizzlies eat just about anything, which means they can live anyplace where there is enough space and enough food.

In the United States, grizzly bears can be found in the area where Montana, Idaho, and Wyoming join together. Yellowstone National Park is in the middle of this area. Grizzly bears also live in Montana in an area that includes Glacier National Park, and in the Selkirk Mountains in Montana and Idaho. In Canada, there are grizzly bears in the forest and mountain areas of Alberta and British Columbia. By far the greatest number of grizzly bears, however, live in northern Canada and Alaska. The best grizzly habitat has very little human activity.

Until human settlements spread across North America, grizzly bears lived throughout the great plains.

Grizzlies and Their Environment

Grizzly bears are a very important part of their environment. Just by eating and looking for food, they do many things to help the plants and animals around them. They provide food for other animals when they leave partly eaten animal scraps. If there is a lot of food, grizzlies will sometimes just eat their favorite part. For example, they will sometimes just eat the fat and eggs of a salmon. The rest of the fish will be left for other animals to finish.

Grizzly bears may also help to prevent the spread of disease by eating dead or sick animals. The digestive system of grizzly bears has adapted so that eating diseased or rotting animal carcasses does not make the bears sick. Grizzlies also reduce the number of insects and rodents in an area.

Grizzly bears help spread plant seeds. When grizzlies eat berries and plants, they knock seeds to the ground. Grizzly bear droppings also help spread seeds. Many seeds pass through the grizzly undigested. These seeds will then be spread to different areas in the grizzly habitat as the bear travels.

The presence of grizzly bears is a sign that a natural environment is healthy. There must be many different types of food in an area if a grizzly is living there. If grizzly bears can find enough food, there is usually more than enough food for other animals.

When grizzly bears dig for roots and insects, they help make seedbeds for new plants to grow.

Viewpoints

Should we set aside more land for grizzly bears?

In many places in North America, governments have set aside land for grizzly bears. National parks, such as Yellowstone National Park in Wyoming, are areas where grizzlies can live without fear of human development destroying their habitat. However, every year bears are killed in national parks if they pose a threat to humans. Grizzly bears living near humans can also cause great damage to farmers' crops and livestock. Bears are increasingly being driven from their homes into smaller areas of isolated wilderness.

PRO

1 Grizzly bears have large home ranges, and need lots of space to survive.

2 If we do not set aside more land for grizzly habitat, the bears may not survive. They have already disappeared from most of their traditional territory.

3 Grizzly bears must eat many different plants and animals, and need a lot of space to find enough to eat. If grizzly bears are not healthy, it may mean that the other animals and plants in the habitat are not healthy and abundant. If people give bears enough space to be healthy, the rest of their environment will probably be well balanced.

CON

1 Humans cannot give up any more of their space for grizzly bears. Grizzlies already have a lot of open spaces in Alaska and northern Canada.

2 If grizzly bears are allowed to move back into their old territories, they will become a danger to humans.

3 Farming and agriculture are very important industries. If the land that is put aside for grizzlies is located too close to farmland, the bears may attack livestock or eat crops. We must protect the agriculture industry.

Grizzlies in the Wild

Grizzlies like to avoid humans as much as they like to avoid other grizzlies. If you are in grizzly bear territory, it is very important to respect the rights of the bears, and not to disturb the area. Unfortunately, most humans do not recognize the markings that are left by bears to warn of their presence.

There are some basic safety rules that you should know if you plan to enter bear country. Always ask park rangers about any grizzly sightings before going camping or hiking. This is especially important if you go into areas where there is not much human activity. Look for signs of fresh tracks, and watch for scratch marks on trees. If you see scratch marks high on a tree, you know a large grizzly has been in the area. Stay away from dead animals. A bear may be returning to eat the animal later, and will be very hostile if it thinks you are trying to steal its food. Always tell a park ranger if you have seen a grizzly bear, or any sign of a grizzly. They can warn other hikers and campers to stay out of the area.

Some grizzly body language is easy to understand. The best way to protect yourself from a grizzly is to learn how to avoid the bears as much as possible.

A Grizzly Quiz

Try this quiz to see how much you know about grizzly bear attacks.
Are the following statements true or false? The answers are
at the bottom of the page.

1 Take your family dog hiking. It will scare away any grizzlies in the area.

2 Make as much noise as possible when you are in grizzly territory.

3 When camping, it is best to store your food in your tent, where grizzly bears cannot get it.

4 Adult grizzlies are dangerous, but bear cubs are cute and harmless.

5 If a grizzly bear is close, run away as fast as possible, or try to climb a tall tree.

6 Not many people get attacked by grizzly bears.

Back country hiking trails sometimes provide racks to hang your food out of a bear's reach.

Answers:

1) False. Dogs will sometimes attract grizzly bears to an area.

2) True. Grizzlies want to avoid humans as much as we want to avoid them. Sing, talk loudly, or ring bells to let bears know of your presence.

3) False. Store any food, or clothes that smell like food, in bear-proof containers, far away from your tent. Park rangers recommend hanging your food containers from a high tree branch.

4) False. Bear cubs are always close to their very protective, aggressive mother. Grizzly mothers can be the most dangerous bears of all.

5) False. Running away can cause a grizzly to chase you, and some grizzly bears can climb trees. The best thing to do is freeze. Try not to stare at the bear, and slowly back away if the grizzly ignores you. If the grizzly approaches, curl up in a ball and cover your head.

6) True. You are more likely to be hit by a bolt of lightning than attacked by a grizzly bear.

Food

Grizzlies need so much food that they spend most of their time either eating or looking for food.

Opposite: Coastal grizzlies are often larger than inland grizzlies because of their rich diet of salmon.

Grizzlies that live near campsites and towns sometimes learn to eat garbage. Once a grizzly has found a garbage dump, it will return to that place year after year, because it is an easy source of food. It is also, however, a dangerous source of food. The more often grizzlies encounter humans, the more likely they are to have conflicts with human populations.

Grizzly bears eat almost everything. They are **omnivores**, which means they eat both plants and animals. They can eat up to 35 pounds (16 kg) of food each day, and almost three times that amount as they prepare to enter their winter dens.

What a grizzly eats depends on where it lives and on the time of year. Grizzlies need so much food that they spend most of their time either eating or looking for food. They have excellent memories, and can remember the locations of good food sources from other years.

Grizzlies are one of the most powerful animals in their environment. Although they are capable of killing large prey, such as moose or elk, grizzly bears eat mostly plants and small animals.

35

How They Hunt

Grizzlies can hunt successfully during the day and the night, although they are usually most active during the day. Despite their enormous size, grizzly bears can run up to 35 miles per hour (56 kph). Their strength, sharp teeth, and claws make them very powerful hunters. With their strong shoulder muscles and paws, a grizzly bear can knock an elk or moose off its feet. With their strong teeth and jaws, grizzlies are able to carry large prey.

Despite their strength and intelligence, grizzlies are not great hunters like wolves or coyotes. Instead of hunting large, healthy, adult animals, they will usually prey on sick or injured animals. They also like to hunt newborn caribou, deer, or elk. **Carrion**, the kill of some other animal, is an easy meal for grizzlies. A grizzly bear will even eat a dead animal that has gone rotten.

Animals that have not survived the winter are an important food source for grizzly bears that have just emerged from their dens. Bears are usually very hungry in the spring. Carrion provides a quick way to build up their strength.

Other Food

Although the grizzly's claws are very sharp and dangerous, they are used more often for digging up roots and insects than for killing large prey. When looking for insect nests, the bears use their claws to turn over rocks and logs. Grizzlies spend hours eating grasses, leaves, roots, seeds, and berries, and they will sometimes kill small animals, such as mice and ground squirrels.

During specific times of the year, some streams are so full of salmon that a grizzly bear can be picky about which fish it wants to eat, and what parts of the fish it prefers.

Grizzlies have a sweet tooth. They love the taste of berries and honey. To get at honey, grizzlies will even attack a beehive that is surrounded by angry bees.

In regions where there is salmon in the rivers, bears are very good at fishing. Different grizzlies have different fishing techniques. Some will sit on the edge of the river and grab the salmon that pass by them. Others will stand on their four legs in the middle of the river and wait until fish swim into their paws and mouths.

Food Sources

Grizzly bears will eat just about anything. What an individual bear eats depends on the food available in its habitat. While inland grizzlies mostly eat plants and other vegetation, coastal grizzlies eat a lot of fish, especially salmon. The grizzly bear's diet also depends on what food is available during different seasons.

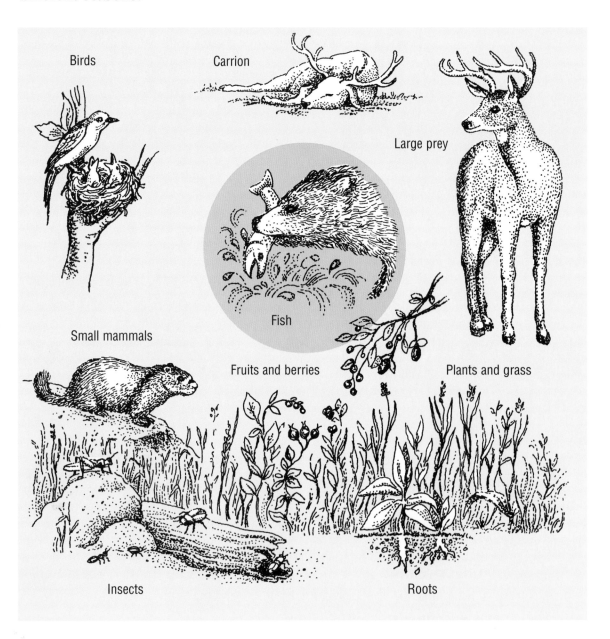

Birds

Carrion

Large prey

Fish

Small mammals

Fruits and berries

Plants and grass

Insects

Roots

Wildlife Biologists Talk About Grizzlies

John A. Murray

"To see a wild bear is always exciting. No other animal so powerfully evokes the North American wilderness."

John A. Murray is a naturalist who has researched and photographed grizzly bears for 18 years. He has written several books on grizzlies, including *Grizzly Bears: an Illustrated Field Guide* and *The Great Bear: Contemporary Writings on the Grizzly.*

Alan Carey

"The grizzly will survive as long as there is a place for him and as long as man lets him survive.... Ultimately, you and I have the final say on the continued existence of this great animal, the grizzly."

Alan Carey is a professional wildlife photographer and researcher who has long been fascinated by grizzly bears. He is author of the book, *In the Path of the Grizzly.*

Frank Craighead

"Alive, the grizzly is a symbol of freedom and understanding— a sign that man can conserve what is left of the earth. Extinct, it will be another fading testimony to things man should have learned more about, but was too preoccupied with himself to notice."

Frank Craighead is a naturalist and author of *Track of the Grizzly.* At one time, he was considered one of the world's leading authorities on the grizzly bears in Yellowstone National Park.

Competition

In Canada and the United States, humans are endangering the existence of the grizzly through poaching and habitat destruction.

Opposite: Although grizzlies will tolerate one another at excellent fishing sources, they will sometimes fight over the best fishing spots.

Finding enough food is essential for a grizzly bear's survival. If a grizzly has not eaten enough during the summer and fall, it will not have enough body fat to live through the winter. Grizzlies like to live in areas that have many different sources of food. Many other animals eat the same foods that grizzly bears eat, but there is usually enough food that competition is not necessary. Male grizzly bears compete with other males during the mating season. By far the most dangerous competitors of the grizzly bear, however, are human beings. In Canada and the United States, humans are endangering the existence of the grizzly through **poaching** and habitat destruction.

In areas such as Yellowstone National Park, bears in search of living space often compete with tourists in search of recreation.

Relationships with Other Animals

Competition between grizzlies is rare. Even though grizzlies sometimes look for food in the same area as other grizzlies, there is usually enough food to avoid competition. If a grizzly is using one food source, the other bear will just move on. Occasionally, fights occur between male grizzlies that are competing for the same female during the mating season, or over food. Male grizzlies will often kill bear cubs so they can mate with the mother. Female bears will not mate and have new cubs until her old cubs are gone. By killing bear cubs, a male grizzly can mate with the female much sooner.

As the biggest, strongest animal in its environment, the grizzly does not face much competition from other animals. If a grizzly is eating in one location, most other animals will avoid that area. Even wolves, intelligent, aggressive hunters that travel in packs, will not usually challenge a full-grown grizzly bear. If they get the chance, wolves or cougars will kill and eat bear cubs, but grizzly mothers are so careful and protective of their young that this does not happen very often.

Wolves are intelligent and powerful hunters, but even they can rarely steal a cub away from its protective mother.

Competing with Humans

Humans and grizzlies compete for territory. Humans are the grizzly bear's worst enemy, and their only serious competition. Human populations require a lot of territory for settlement, industry, and recreation. As human activities move into grizzly territories, grizzlies are forced out. Grizzly bears survive best when they have little or no contact with humans.

Grizzly bears are sometimes shot because they are too close to homes, ranches, farms, or hiking areas. Since grizzlies have only one or two cubs every three or four years, it takes a long time to replace killed grizzlies.

Many problems between humans and grizzlies result when disappearing habitat forces grizzlies to turn to human sources for food. These cubs are raiding a campsite in Yellowstone National Park.

Decline in Population

There are three main reasons for the decline in grizzly bear populations: hunting, poaching, and habitat loss.

Hunting

Hunting grizzly bears is allowed in many places. Governments are usually very careful about how many bears can be killed each year, and make hunters buy licenses to hunt grizzlies. Bears are hunted for many reasons. Governments sometimes allow grizzly hunts if there are too many bears in one area. Hunters consider the grizzly to be a valuable prize because of its size and strength.

Poaching

Sometimes grizzlies are killed by people who are hunting for sport, but who do not have a license. This type of illegal hunting is called poaching. Grizzly bears are sometimes made into trophies for display, including mounted bear heads, hides, or bear paws. Sometimes grizzly parts are made into jewelry or ashtrays. Many people around the world will pay a lot of money for these items. Some people believe that they become stronger if they own a piece of such a powerful animal. In certain cultures, some grizzly bear body parts, such as the gallbladder and the paws, are believed to have magical powers and are used in medicines. Poachers often kill grizzly bears so they can make money selling these body parts.

At one time, hunting grizzly bears was a very popular pastime. The size and power of the grizzly made it a prized trophy.

Habitat Loss

Habitat loss is the greatest threat to grizzly bears. Historically, brown bears lived throughout much of the wilderness areas of North America. Grizzlies once lived on the plains. In the nineteenth and twentieth centuries, most of these bears were killed by humans out of fear, for food, for sport, or because they interfered with land settlement.

Today, the grizzly is gone from most of its traditional territory in the United States and in southern Canada. As human populations continue to move into grizzly territory, the bears are forced into areas that do not have enough food, or into spaces that bring them in more contact with humans.

Grizzly bears have lost 98 percent of their traditional range south of the United States-Canada border.

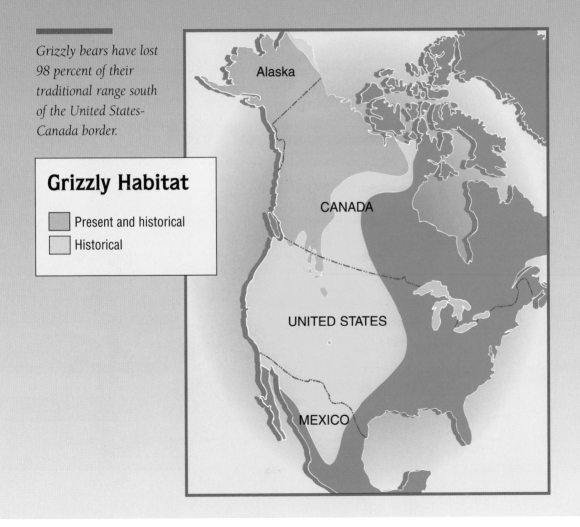

Grizzly Habitat

Present and historical
Historical

Folklore

For centuries, bears have played a large part in the folklore of many cultures. Many different cultures have told stories about the resemblance between humans and a bear standing on its hind feet. Brown bears appear in many well-known stories.

Usually, bears are portrayed in folklore as intelligent, strong, and fair. Many stories describe grizzlies as mysterious. A few describe the bear as vicious and frightening. Many North American Aboriginal cultures consider the bear to be a sacred animal. Their stories often show admiration for the bear's powerful spirit.

Opposite: In the nineteenth century, grizzly bears were often portrayed as vicious killers that would attack humans for no reason.

Drawings of bears were made by Aboriginal peoples in New Mexico throughout the tenth to twelfth centuries. Most North American Aboriginal peoples had great respect for bears, which they felt were very similar to humans.

Folklore History

Ancient Greeks and Romans thought the bear was very compassionate. Bears were often associated with nurses. This was probably because of the mother bear's well-known devotion to her cubs. The ancient Greeks named two very popular constellations after myths that are based on the bear. The Big Dipper forms the tail of Ursa Major, or the Great Bear, and the Little Dipper forms Ursa Minor, or the Little Bear.

The grizzly bear is very important in the stories of North American Aboriginal peoples. Many of their tales are about bears raising children and healing people. Medicine healers would use parts of the grizzly to treat illnesses. Grizzly bears were thought to have powerful spirits, so after killing grizzlies, it was common to apologize to the bear's spirit, and have a ceremony to honor the bear. Many Aboriginal cultures call the grizzly bear "grandfather" or "brother" out of respect. The Blackfoot people have so much respect for the grizzly that they will not even say its name out loud.

According to ancient Greek mythology, the god Zeus turned a woman, Callisto, into Ursa Major in order to protect her from his jealous wife. Callisto's son, Arcas, did not recognize his mother, and tried to kill her. Zeus then turned Arcas into Ursa Minor. The long tails of the two bears were stretched as Zeus pulled them into the sky.

Myths vs. Facts

Grizzlies attack people for no reason.

Grizzlies go out of their way to avoid humans. Grizzly attacks usually only occur when humans enter grizzly habitats, or when a female grizzly believes her cubs are in danger.

Grizzlies are lazy and slow.

Grizzly bears often move slowly, spending most of their day eating plants and insects. They can, however, run at speeds up to 35 miles per hour (58 kph).

Grizzly bears cannot climb trees.

Although grizzly cubs climb trees in play, or in times of danger, adult bears do not often climb trees. Grizzlies can, however, pull themselves up a tree just like humans can.

Grizzlies kill their enemies with a "bear hug."

Bears sometimes seem to be hugging their prey, but they are usually just holding it in a better position to use their powerful jaws and claws.

Folktales

In folklore, bears are described in many different ways—sometimes cruel and stupid, and sometimes loving and intelligent. Here are a few stories you might enjoy reading:

Magical Bears

Learn about the value of friendship and how the Ursa Major constellation, which contains the Big Dipper, was created from a dancing bear.

Czernecki, Stefan and Rhodes, Timothy. *Bear in the Sky.* Winnipeg: Hyperion Press, 1990.

Hibernating Bears

A grizzly bear steals the warm wind that brings spring in this delightful tale that explains why bears hibernate during the winter.

Fraser, Frances. *The Bear Who Stole the Chinook.* Vancouver: Douglas & McIntyre, 1990.

Spirit Grizzlies

"The Grizzly and the Rattlesnake Men" is a myth from the Pacific Northwest. It tells the story of a grizzly bear that acts as a spirit guide to help save a young girl from a mysterious illness.

Matson, Emerson N. *Longhouse Legends.* Toronto: Thomas Nelson and Sons, 1968.

Half-bear/Half-man

This adaptation of a Russian folktale tells about an honest creature who is half-man, half-bear, and how he outwits an evil witch.

Kimmel, Eric A. and Mikolaycak, Charles. *Bearhead.* New York: Holiday House, 1991.

Mothering Bears

"The Bearchild" is one of many tales that tells of a mother bear raising a human child. In this story, the child has a difficult time when it returns to live with humans.

Fiddler, Chief Thomas. *Legends From The Forest.* Moonbeam, Ontario: Penumbra Press, 1985.

Powerful Bears

An elder must choose a name for his strong, healthy grandson. After telling the story of a powerful grizzly that attacked one of his people, the elder surprises his community by naming his grandson after that worthy opponent.

Craigan, Charlie, illustrator. Based on a legend of the Sechelt People. *Mayuk the Grizzly Bear.* Gibsons, British Columbia: Nightwood Editions, 1993.

In "How the Old Man Created the World," an old man creates the grizzly bear, but makes it too strong and too large. The old man must then go live high up in the mountains to avoid the grizzly.

Curry, Jane Louise. *Back in the Beforetime.* New York: Margaret K. McElderry Books, 1987.

Grizzly Bear Populations

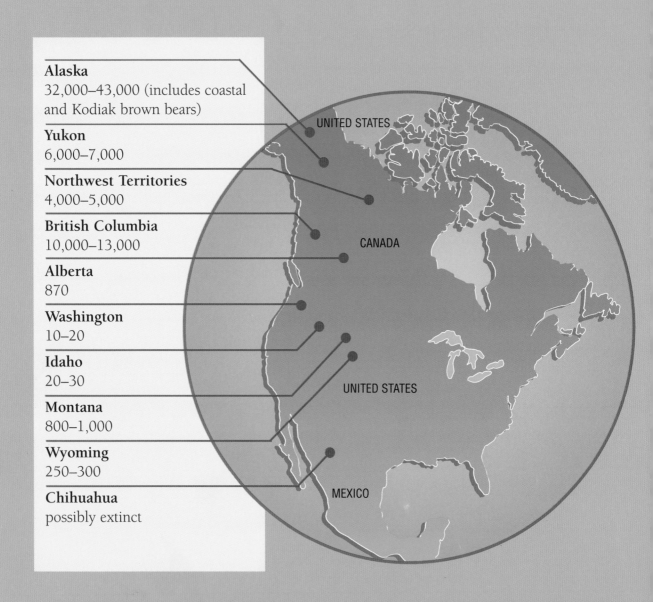

Alaska
32,000–43,000 (includes coastal and Kodiak brown bears)

Yukon
6,000–7,000

Northwest Territories
4,000–5,000

British Columbia
10,000–13,000

Alberta
870

Washington
10–20

Idaho
20–30

Montana
800–1,000

Wyoming
250–300

Chihuahua
possibly extinct

UNITED STATES

CANADA

UNITED STATES

MEXICO

Status

The grizzly subspecies is considered to be threatened in the United States, and vulnerable in Canada.

Grizzly bears once lived throughout the western half of North America, from Alaska down to Mexico. The grizzly has since disappeared from most of its former habitat in the United States, except in Alaska. While brown bears are quite common in other parts of the world, the grizzly subspecies is considered to be **threatened** in the United States, and **vulnerable** in Canada. This means the grizzly may be endangered if there is further poaching and habitat loss.

Worldwide Brown Bear Populations			
Country	**Status**	**Country**	**Status**
Albania	unknown	Japan	3,000
Bulgaria	700–750	Lebanon	possibly extinct
Canada	22,500	Mexico	possibly extinct
China	unknown	Mongolia	unknown
Commonwealth	118,000	Norway	160–230
Former Czechoslovakia	700	Pakistan	fewer than 200
Democratic People's Republic of Korea	uncommon	Poland	70–75
Finland	450	Romania	6,300
France	20–30	Spain	115
Greece	fewer than 100	Sweden	500–700
India	rare	Syria	few
Iran	few	Turkey	common
Iraq	few	United States	44,000
Italy	60–70	former Yugoslavia	1,600–2,000

Protecting Grizzlies

Many steps have been taken to prevent the grizzly bear from disappearing in the United States and in Canada. In North America, it is illegal to buy or sell the parts of a protected animal without a special license. In spite of these laws, poachers still kill some grizzly bears and sell their body parts.

To protect grizzlies, it is important to protect the land in which grizzlies live. Grizzly bear reserves have been set up in many national, state, and provincial parks. These areas limit human activity so that the bears may live in peace. One of the biggest dangers to grizzly bears is for the bears to become used to humans, human food, and garbage as a food source. These grizzlies often have to be shot because they become a danger to humans. National and provincial parks and campgrounds have very strict rules about how and where to store food, and how to enjoy wilderness areas without damaging it. These rules help to protect bears as well as humans. Despite all of these efforts, many people think the grizzly will soon exist only in Alaska and northern Canada.

National parks often use food to trap and move bears that are too close to human areas. Some bears must be trapped and moved many times, since they often travel long distances to return to their home range.

Viewpoints

Should people be allowed to hunt grizzly bears?

In many parts of North America, it is legal to hunt grizzly bears with a license from the government. Some people believe that hunting grizzly bears is a way to control bear populations and make money for local people and the government. Others believe that hunting threatens the grizzly's survival.

PRO

1 Grizzly bear hunting is limited by the government so that only a few bears are killed each year. Hunting bears is a challenging sport that is carefully controlled by the government.

2 The government makes money from the licenses sold to bear hunters. This money can be put into grizzly management programs. Many Aboriginal peoples, especially in the North, can also make money from hunters. This makes the bears a valuable resource for local people.

3 A grizzly bear hunt is necessary when there are too many bears in an area. Hunting some grizzlies can benefit other bears by allowing them more space and food.

CON

1 Grizzly bears have disappeared from their range in much of North America, primarily because of humans. If we are to help grizzlies survive, hunting must not be allowed.

2 Hunters sometimes sell the body parts of grizzly bears that are legally hunted. This may increase the demand for these items, which may increase poaching.

3 Many people believe that humans have no right to kill any wild animals. They believe bears have a right to live peacefully in their habitat.

Grizzlies in the Wild

There are many places in North America where you can go to see grizzly bears in the wild. Here are just a few:

Khutzeymateen/K'tzim-a-Deen River Sanctuary

The Khutzeymateen River Sanctuary is a 171 square mile (443 sq km) area of land in British Columbia, Canada. In 1992 this land was officially put aside as grizzly habitat, ending a 20-year fight to save the area from clear-cut logging. There are believed to be around 50 grizzlies living in the sanctuary. The area is managed in part by the Tsimshian people who have lived in the Khutzeymateen area for centuries. It is possible to go on guided bear tours of the Khutzeymateen. For more information, write to:

Khutzeymateen River Sanctuary
c/o Valhalla Society
Box 329
New Denver, BC
V0G 1S0 Canada

Denali National Park and Preserve

Denali National Park in Alaska is believed to have 200 to 300 grizzly bears living in its boundaries. Hiking and camping permits are necessary if you plan to visit the area. For more information, write to:

Denali National Park
and Preserve
P.O. Box 9
Denali Park, AK
99755

Khutzeymateen River Sanctuary

A mother grizzly and her two cubs in Denali National Park and Preserve.

McNeil River State Wildlife Sanctuary

One of the best places to see grizzly bears in the wild is at the McNeil River State Wildlife Sanctuary. At the McNeil waterfalls, you can often see up to 100 bears at a time, all fishing for salmon. Human activity is kept to a minimum in the sanctuary. Land development, hunting, and trapping are not allowed. Great care is taken to see that humans do not disturb the bears. Since the beginnings of the Sanctuary, more than 20 years ago, there have been no bear attacks, nor has any bear needed to be destroyed.

To see the bears, you must first enter a lottery. Only the few lottery winners are allowed into the reserve each year. Bear experts are available to answer any of the visitors' questions. For more information on McNeil River State Wildlife Sanctuary, and how to enter the lottery, write to:

McNeil River State Wildlife Sanctuary
c/o Alaska Department of Fish and Game
333 Raspberry Road
Anchorage, AK
99518

What You Can Do

There are many ways to support efforts to help grizzly bears survive in their natural habitat. Many conservation groups are devoted to helping this magnificent animal. Write to one to get more information, and to see what you can do to help grizzly bears.

Conservation Groups

INTERNATIONAL

International Union for Conservation of Nature and Natural Resources (IUCN)
World Conservation Union
28, rue Mauverney
CH-1196 Gland
Switzerland

International Association for Bear Research and Management
c/o Sterling Miller
Alaska Department of Fish and Game
333 Raspberry Rd.
Anchorage, AK
99518

UNITED STATES

Greater Yellowstone Coalition
P.O. Box 1874
13 South Willson Ave.
Bozeman, MT
59715

Great Bear Foundation
P.O. Box 1289
Bozeman, MT
59771
(The Great Bear Foundation publishes a quarterly magazine called *Bear News* that contains information about bear conservation. For more information, write: Bear News, Great Bear Foundation, Box 1289, Bozeman, MT, 59715)

North American Bear Society
3875 N. 44th Street
Suite 102
Phoenix, AZ
85018

Wildlife Conservation Society
185th Street and Southern Boulevard
Bronx, NY
10460

CANADA

Canadian Wildlife Federation
2740 Queensview Drive
Ottawa, Ontario
K2B 1A2

Twenty Fascinating Facts

1 Grizzly bears have an excellent sense of smell. Some say a grizzly can smell certain roots that are buried under several inches of soil, or even a stick of chewing gum that is in the glove compartment of an automobile.

2 You can tell how old a grizzly is by looking at one of its teeth. Scientists remove a grizzly's tooth and look at it under a microscope. Like tree rings, grizzly teeth add a ring for every year of the bear's life.

3 Despite their size, grizzlies can walk silently through a forest. This is why it is so important to make a lot of noise to alert the bear of your presence. You will probably not hear the bear before it will hear you.

4 Grizzlies can run at speeds up to 35 miles per hour (56 kph).

5 Grizzly bears are excellent swimmers, and sometimes they swim just for enjoyment.

6 Grizzlies will ignore the stings of angry bees just to get some honey from a beehive.

11 Grizzly bears like to eat garbage because it requires little effort. They will remember the location of garbage dumps and will often return to those areas year after year.

12 During long, cold winters, grizzlies can spend up to 8 months in their winter den.

13 Before they enter their winter dens, grizzlies have often eaten so much that they have a layer of fat several inches deep.

14 Grizzly bears have long, sharp claws that are used more often for digging up plants and insects than for killing large prey.

15 During their winter sleep, which can last several months, grizzlies do not eat, drink, or eliminate waste.

7 Although grizzlies usually avoid other grizzlies, they will often gather at a particularly good food source. Up to 15 grizzlies have been seen in one area of a stream during salmon season.

9 A grizzly's paws help to cool the bear down in hot weather. Grizzlies do not have sweat glands, so they rest their pads on the ground to help cool the rest of their bodies.

8 Most grizzly bears are brown, but they can also be cream-colored or almost black. A grizzly's fur can change color from year to year.

10 If there is a lot of food, grizzly bears will sometimes eat just the parts of an animal that contain the most fat and nutrients. Other animals often eat the rest.

16 Although adult grizzlies rarely climb trees, cubs are very good climbers. They climb trees both in play and when their mother warns them of danger.

17 Cubs weigh only a fraction of what adult grizzlies weigh. They will gain hundreds of pounds in their first few years.

18 If a pregnant grizzly mother is not fat enough before she goes into a den for the winter, she will not give birth to her cubs. She will mate again the next year.

19 Some people will pay a lot of money for a grizzly bear's gallbladder, which certain cultures use in medicine.

20 At one time, grizzly bears lived all over the western half of North America, from Alaska down to Mexico.

Glossary

camouflage: When an animal's appearance blends in with its environment so that it is very difficult to see

carrion: The flesh of a dead animal

delayed implantation: A process by which an unborn animal does not begin to grow right away in its mother's womb

gestation period: The length of time that a female is pregnant

grizzled: Sprinkled or streaked with white or gray

guard hairs: The long, straight, coarse hairs that lie over the underfur of an animal

hibernation: A period of time during the winter when certain animals' body temperature and heart rate drop dramatically in order to conserve energy

home range: The entire area in which a grizzly bear lives

molt: When an animal loses its old coat of winter fur, and replaces it with a lighter coat of fur for the summer

nonretractable: When some things, especially claws, are permanently in an outstretched position. Cats have retractable claws that return back into the paw when not in use.

omnivores: Animals that eat both plants and other animals

poaching: Killing an animal illegally

threatened: A species that is declining in numbers, and may soon become endangered or extinct if no action is taken by humans to help it

underfur: The soft, short layer of hair that lies close to an animal's skin

vulnerable: A species that could easily become threatened or endangered if it is not protected

weaned: When a mother animal feeds less and less of her milk to her young. The young are usually eating other food at this point.

Suggested Reading

Brown, Gary. *The Great Bear Almanac*. New York: Lyons & Burford, 1993.

Herrero, Steven. *Bear Attacks: Their Causes and Avoidance*. New York: Nick Lyons Books, 1985.

Lynch, Wayne. *Bears*. Vancouver: Douglas & McIntyre, 1993.

Murray, John A. *Grizzly Bears: An Illustrated Field Guide*. Boulder: Roberts Rinehart, 1995.

Nentl, Jerolyn Ann. *The Grizzly*. Mankato: Crestwood House, 1984.

Olsen, Lance. *Field Guide to the Grizzly Bear*. Seattle: Sasquatch Books, 1992.

Patent, Dorothy Hinshaw. *The Way of the Grizzly*. New York: Clarion Books, 1987.

Stirling, Ian, ed. *Bears: Majestic Creatures of the Wild*. New York: Rodale Press, 1993.

Stone, Lynn M. *Grizzlies*. Minneapolis: Carolrhoda Books, Inc., 1993.

Index

AUG

1998